THE LAST PETAL

PARI MODANI

For my unpoppable bubbles.

Your smiling faces melt my heart.

Contents

Contents

Introduction

This is my first ever book so I'm kind of nervous, as I should be, I guess, but here goes nothing.

The settings of the places when/where I write are no sandy beaches with a beautiful sky overhead or a hidden valley somewhere in between snow-capped mountain or a garden with a stretch of aromatized flowers. Not so fairy-tale-like. It's more like on the desks of my school, inside my bedroom and even in the bathroom when I'm scrubbing my teeth or my skin. There are no boundaries to the venues. Plain, old, simple and sober.

Laughing-face-emoji

Words fill up my head and flow out in the form of thoughts and I try my best to ink them on paper before I lose track of them. They never let me down and cling to me like my own flesh.

The Last Petal compiles most of my possessions and is as diverse as the human race. Nature, stupid-but-worthy teenage thoughts, desires, monsters, etcetera, etcetera, etcetera.

There are no limits. There never will be.

These were my hold-to-when-down words and I pray they stay stuck in your head as much as they in mine.

Enjoy.

With the sweetness of your coffee,

Pari O_o

Acknowledgements

There are just so many people I should be giving the credits to and it would never be enough.

Firstly, I'd like to thank Kalyan Kumar for supporting me through the publishing of the book and being there for my endless stupid questions. In addition, I would like to thank his team I was left unaware of.

Thank you Amma- Appa for nodding your head and making this one worth all the headaches you gave me and I gave you.

Laughing-face-emoji

All I ever wanted is that proud smile I get from you when I score good grades but this time it could be for this book.

Fingers-crossed

Thank you, my 4 Pandava-s, for staying aloof but always around when the thoughts hit me and I had a messy trouble in my head so my words didn't make sense. You guys suck sometimes but awesome otherwise and that's the best part of it.

Thank you, Panda, for noticing the potential in me and pushing me for this. Remember the favour you asked for? Here's one, and I will try to make it more. You rock our worlds.

Thank you, Nobi, for stealing my papers where I had my drafts and reading them off. I never knew how you got your hands on them, you're weirdly different.

Thank you Anv for forcing up the ideas I thought I'd never have done by myself and supporting me by always sticking by my side no matter what. I adore you, always.

Thank you Ani, for being there even when you were not and for all the hype. Your existence always mattered, even if I didn't get to see you through my eyes.

You guys bring out the best of me.

Thank you to all those who believed in me, as well as all those who didn't because your criticism never really helped anyone.

At last, thank you to all my precious readers for spending your valuable time reading.

I'm honoured to have you as my audience.

Author

Pari Modani was born to creative and curious parents who passed their interests upon her, along came the passion she saw them working with since her childhood. Jumping from one city to another, she now resides in the Pink City: Jaipur, Rajasthan.

Pari tries to express herself through art such as poetry, sketches and doodles since explaining via words is not something she considers herself good at. She claims pen and paper as her forever companions.

"The Last Petal" is the debut of Pari Modani which contains a collection of poems on versatile topics. Directly from the notes, she quotes.

Tricks

You look uninterested

The way you're looking away

But I know that's just a trick

To sweep me up from the floor again.

You try to act like it's obvious

When there's everything you can change,

But you sit still and smile to nowhere

Because if you're caught red handed,

There'll be a mess we'd create.

Keeping all that in mind,

A smile passes my face

Because I would say this to nobody else

But a picture of you that's kept far away.

Lullaby

The clock ticks above my head.

Unlike everything else, time never had an end.

I find myself sleepless,

Twisting and turning, irritated by the sound.

My mind's occupied with thoughts.

Thoughts I shouldn't have.

But who would stop a stubborn monster

To do what it wants?

I shut my eyes but it helps no more.

The monster didn't get what it wanted,

Now it won't let go.

I wish they could sing me a lullaby.

I wish I would've snatched

The opportunity when I had

Cause life's so uncertain

And even though the monster is selfish,

It does whatever it can until death.

Shiny Stars

I like the glow in your eyes when the stars shine.

Piece Of Me

It's in my heart, my head, my soul.

It's everywhere I look,

It's everything I feel,

It resides in every cell, every atom of my body.

It's a part of me that I cannot escape.

It's in my past, my future,

And in my present continuous tense.

Festive

Sometimes things are not all firecrackers and party poppers,

Sometimes they are more like blood pressure high due to stress
and all the chaos caused because you're getting prepared for the
festival.

Sometimes things are not rangolis and laddus,

Sometimes they are "oh my god, I wish nobody was feeling missed
out."

Sometimes things are not a glitter mess, fancy dress,

Sometimes they are a mess of clothes and work overload.

And that's what makes it special.

When you break through a routine

And take a deep breath, look around to find

Cheerful faces that melt your heart right away.

Numbness

"You'll eventually understand what you want to do after the numbness, it's the way of the universe."

Vexation

I stay happy

Probably forever.

Soon my smile goes down,

Now mood doesn't matter.

It's not always about myself

Yet I've a reason to be sad.

The world that surrounds us,

Doesn't it make you mad?!

Going into the deep thinking

Of all the sorrows and misery,

You'll feel that yourself

Isn't it a true thing to worry?

The Book On My Desk

I'm in love

I agree,

Not with the mammals

The creator set free.

I fell in love

With its scent

It's sentence,

The thoughts, I feel.

That residence of magic

Never let me down.

The only place where

My heart's peace is found.

I fell in love

With its touch,

It's words,

The emotions, I feel.

Crown

She stood strong

With her head raised high,

But had to bow down

When the king passed by.

"No Please!

Your crown will fall!"

Cried some voice,

Mysterious to all.

At that instance,

A promise was made.

She shall never bow down

For her dignity to be stayed.

Aimless

Mortals have no idea

What they're doing

But they let it sink in

And do it anyways.

Father

A person to go to at all times,

The one who cherishes me once in a while.

So very loving and really kind.

Oh father, you're a jewel of every child!

You stay swamped

Taking care of all our needs,

But you also play with me

Whenever you get free.

Be the Daddy's Princess, as they say,

And I'll walk with pride.

I'm your permanent follower.

Thy cake of advices never gets over.

In your formal words,

Here's a gigantic toast

To all the stars just like you,

Oh, dear father, I love you!

Expiry

Oh, how do we ever lose people?

Do you even know?

My mistake, your mistake?

One in ego, another in hope. Wow

And when does it get back to normal?

When ego dies or hope finds courage?

No, my fellows, it does never,

Maybe when people attain knowledge.

Of the emotions, world and human race,

They'll find a way to apologise

But it would always be late,

Thinking they'd ever concise.

The memories, moments of all days,

Wanting to relive them once again.

Oh man, it was a story from past,

Now ignoring it for the hurt they gain.

Sit Next To Me

Sit next to me

For when you're also tried to speak,

For when you've attention to seek,

For no reason at all.

Unplanned Plans

Never aim for it,

Shall the vibe match

We may fall in love

After days of friendship.

Shall the fight outbreak

We may lose

The love birds as well.

Shall we save the lives

Of blood wanting enemies

And create a bond unbroken.

You, me, never know.

Mortals confined by destiny?

Weightage

People say certain words so carelessly as if they carry weightage none.

Love.

Hate.

Trust.

Doubt.

Rental

It's an illusion

They don't understand.

We're not perfect,

We've got flaws in my head.

It's all in their head.

Yeah, they don't understand

We're not permanent, instead

It's rental.

We're rental residents.

Breaking Muscles

I gave him my heart.

He tossed it,

Dropped it on the ground,

It didn't break.

He pushed in a knife,

No muscle bleeded.

But then he started to walk away,

leaving my heart on the ground.

The view got my heart breaking

Into pieces never to be found.

Mistakes

It's life, shit happens.

We make mistakes

To realise it was a mistake

To learn from it.

Chill.

Eagle Claws

If it were ever legal

To perform some stunts

Not by myself,

But with others,

Then I would own a golden eagle

Who has claws to snatch eyes,

Beak to break and bite

The tongue and skin

Of the mentally feeble.

Never Knew

You never know how beautiful smart is.

Trapped

Like a bird in a cage

Weeping for freedom

And flight in the air,

The sadness turned into rage,

Tears to fire,

So, it set out

To find a passage

From between the bars.

Squeezing little to more,

Adjusting the ribcage

As it slowly came out

Flapping its wings, it hit me:

Victory and freedom

Didn't bound by age.

Animals

Let the dogs bark,

Let the snakes hiss,

Let the chameleons change colours to grab your attention,

You do you; you stay aloof.

A Picture Of You

The ice doesn't break

But there would be quiet

If the clock doesn't tick so loud

On a rainy winter night.

My thoughts trapped in my head,

Trembling between the eyes two

And I end up convincing myself

To talk to a picture of you.

Grow

Day to moonlight,

Water to clouds,

There's this infinity

That has never been found.

Unwatched places,

Untasted flavours,

Minds full of wild,

Hearts full of colours.

Playing with time,

Words form the tragic,

So, let's grow together,

Together, with this magic.

Explana

Why care explain when

"I don't want to" is a reason good enough?

The Rose Petals In The Curb

The trees blossom like a flower in the sky.

Sleeping beauty got to waste a lot of time,

But when the moon will shine

After the harsh of daylight,

There'll be birds that sing

To quiet the children who cry.

What if the queen has prince

Not the king to satisfy?

Ring around the roses could be the guide.

Not everyone has life miserable like mine.

But when the queen sits down,

It's the utmost delight,

Cause the followers she preaches

Bring the trees to the sky.

Venom

Dudes and divas,

Girls and guys,

Brides with grooms

Living a vicious life.

One little spoon of potion in the curd-

Hundreds of ways to kill a person.

A naked bed that got wet.

A bloody door painted in red.

Walls and ceilings narrated the story

Of the screams of the dishes

Cracking up at jokes about the ring.

Faint pretty lights,

Crushed scented flowers.

The tree knew Romeo and Juliet,

Even after the death,

Were meant to be together.

Goodness

I'm purely of the opinion

Good stories, good memories,

Good people, good food

Could never be placed

In six closed walls

Of the speech.

Mere Myths

I grew up to realise hell and heaven were mere myths.

When Peace Is A Sin

I searched for one sin

And I found it with you.

So, I handed you my days

Signed my nights to your names,

Showered thou with

My precious time.

Peace was that sin,

The one that detached me

From everyone but you.

You Served me my sin,

I played with time at thy will.

Flowers And Leaves

It's easy to love a flower,

Beautiful, scented,

Like no other.

It's tough to love a leaf,

Ordinary, green, the ones

That shatter your belief.

Motive

"What's the motive?"

I scream to the universe.

I'm not included in the matrix

Nor I could run away from it.

I feel like I'm interested

In too much to have

My decision on one.

There's too much on the plate

To be overlooked.

Yet there's not time enough

To gaze at it all.

"What's the motive?

I scream to my reflection

In the mirror, the part of me

That smiles not knowing

What it feels like.

Bad Days

Each day might not be yours.

Today you might want to be stuck at your sadness.

Appreciate the bad days, darling.

Voices

They speak of the sweet, man,

They speak of sorrow.

Even at the time of silence,

There's a voice that fills the hollow.

Search in the deep,

Search at heights, young lad,

For where now peace resides,

There was once noise.

Monster

There was no monster

When there was no light.

There was no monster

In the pitch black

I ran to leave behind.

The monster was in me,

At the back of my head.

Snow And Hail

Snow and hail,

So much alike,

Yet so apart.

Like sunrises and sunsets,

Cheerful and pleasing,

But always stay aloof

From the other.

Snow and hail.

Snow is you,

Hail, I am.

Pretty we are when different,

Ugly it gets when together.

Just like the match

Of rain and winds

Create a storm,

When you and I collide,

We create destruction none alike.

We, snow and hail.

Interlocked

Summer sun,

Monsoon clouds,

Winter breeze,

Spring bees,

The combinations terrify me.

Like the addition is harmful

But when subtracted from another,

Changes the entire value.

Though I can't believe

These ones fit together

Flawless like the last piece of puzzle.

Uncaged

I'm a free bird,

Not capable to lock

In the boundaries

Of a cage.

Head Over Heels

Head over heels about small things,

Music?

Chocolates?

Greens?

Sunsets?

Moonlight?

Yes please!

Getting head over heels about small things

Since they provide the most pleasure.

Differences

Pessimism is different from realism.

Optimism is different from positivity.

Peace is different from silence.

Scars is different from those harms.

Doing is different from thinking.

Should is different from have to.

Looking fool is different from being fool.

Teasing is different from bullying.

Opinions is different from Respect.

Want to is different from must.

Politeness is different from friendliness.

I said what I said.

Chaos

Mornings bloom with chaos in my head.

A really nice nightmare disturbed my sweet sleep-in bed.

The Absence

Their presence seems meaningless

To us when they're around.

We don't notice they've

Became a part of our habits now.

Then when they'll vanish

From our worlds, it would be

Strange and hollow.

Let the future be, I say,

Even the idea of it

Shakes the land below my feet.

As the old man says "Every ending ends up being a new beginning.",

Connect with the author on their voyage.

Instagram~ parimodani